Your Faith
SIKHISM

By *Harriet Brundle*

You can find the **bold** words in this book in the Glossary on page 24.

PHOTO CREDITS

Photocredits: Abbreviations: l-left, r-right, b-bottom, t-top, c-centre, m-middle. All images are courtesy of Shutterstock.com.
Front Cover,1 – Shutterstock mixed & India Picture. 2 – f9photos. 3 – India Picture. 4 – naluwan. 5 – Denis Tabler. 6 – India Picture. 7 – India Picture. 8 – szefei. 9 – LoloStock. 10 – Tukaram Karve. 11 – India Picture. 12 – Asaf Eliason. 13l – saiko3p. 13r – 1970s. 14 – f9photos. 15 – Elena Mirage. 16 – Andrew Park. 17 – Jultud. 18l – Dmitry Kalinovsky. 18r – litchima. 19tr – Polryaz. 19l – Coprid. 19br – ermess. 20 – India Picture. 21 – India Picture. 22 – India Picture. 23 – saiko3p

CONTENTS

©2016
Book Life
King's Lynn
Norfolk PE30 4LS

ISBN: 978-1-910512-92-0

Written by:
Harriet Brundle

Designed by:
Matt Rumbelow

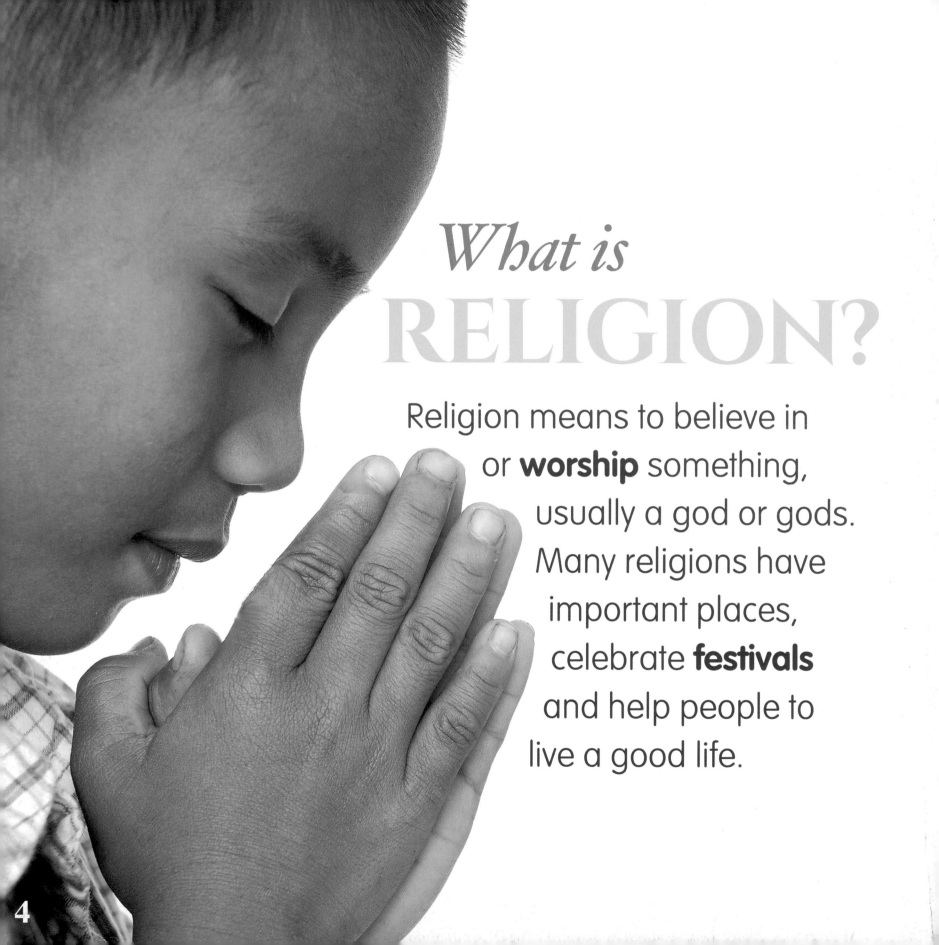

What is
RELIGION?

Religion means to believe in or **worship** something, usually a god or gods. Many religions have important places, celebrate **festivals** and help people to live a good life.

There are lots of different religions. Some of the religions with the largest amount of followers are Christianity, Islam, Hinduism and Sikhism.

CHRISTIANITY

ISLAM

HINDUISM

SIKHISM

What is SIKHISM?

Sikhism is a religion that began over five hundred years ago. It is the fifth largest religion in the world.

People who follow Sikhism are called Sikhs. Sikhism was started by a man called Guru Nanak.

The word Guru means teacher.

The Ten GURUS

Sikh people believe that Guru Nanak was the first guru and after him there were nine other human gurus. The ten gurus created the religion of Sikhism.

The gurus taught people how to live a good life and become close to God.

The Guru
GRANTH
SAHIB

The Guru Granth Sahib is a special book for Sikhs. It is important because they believe it is the eleventh guru and contains the words of the ten human gurus.

Written as lots of different **hymns**, the Guru Granth Sahib helps Sikhs follow their religion.

PLACES OF WORSHIP

A Sikh place of worship is called a gurdwara. Anywhere can be a gurdwara, as long as the Guru Granth Sahib is there and it is shown respect.

Many larger gurdwaras have tall flag poles on the roof that show the Sikh flag. When at a gurdwara, Sikh people read and sing hymns from the Guru Granth Sahib.

Gurdwara

Sikh flag pole

The Golden TEMPLE

The most special gurdwara for Sikhs is called The Golden Temple. It is in the country of India.

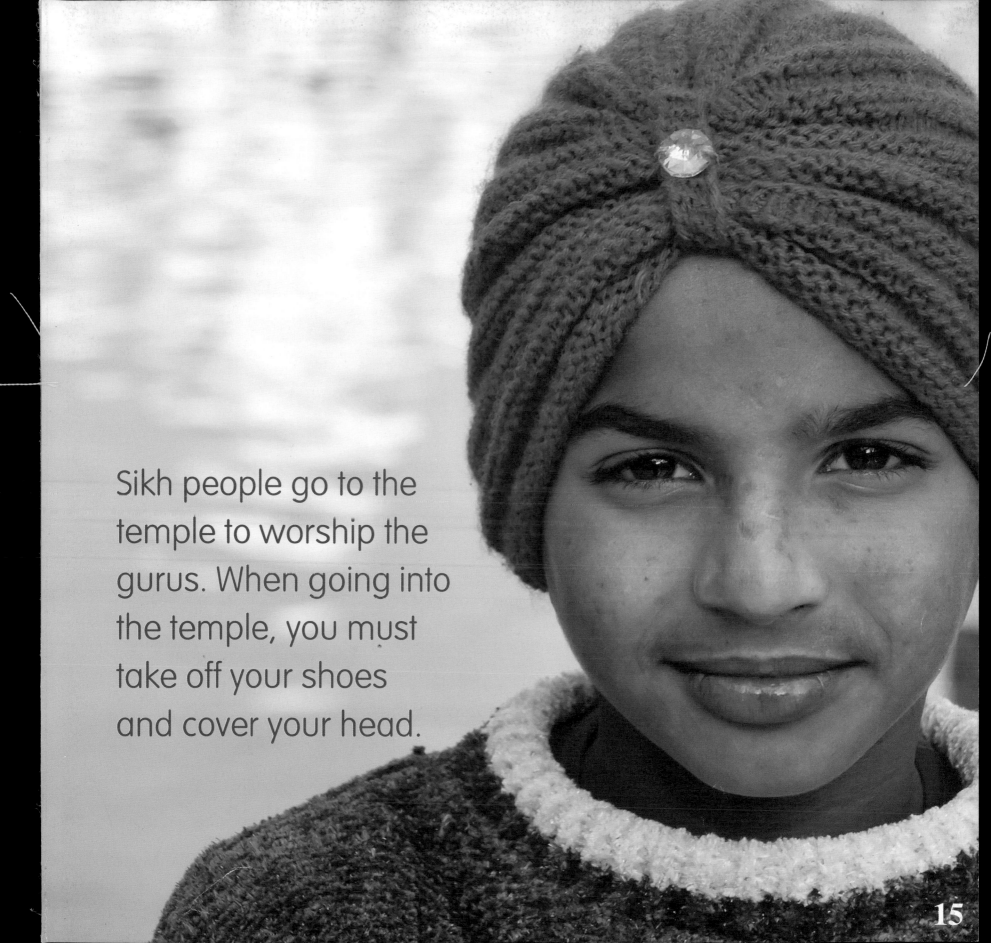

Sikh people go to the temple to worship the gurus. When going into the temple, you must take off your shoes and cover your head.

Amrit CEREMONY

Sikh people can take Amrit, a special **ceremony** that must be done in front of five other Sikhs. Parts of the Guru Granth Sahib are read and prayers are said.

A mixture of sugar and water called Amrit is drunk. A Sikh who has taken Amrit is called a Khalsa.

The FIVE K's

It is important to Sikh people to have the five K's with them all the time. *The five K's are:*

1. kes uncut hair

2. kanga
a wooden comb

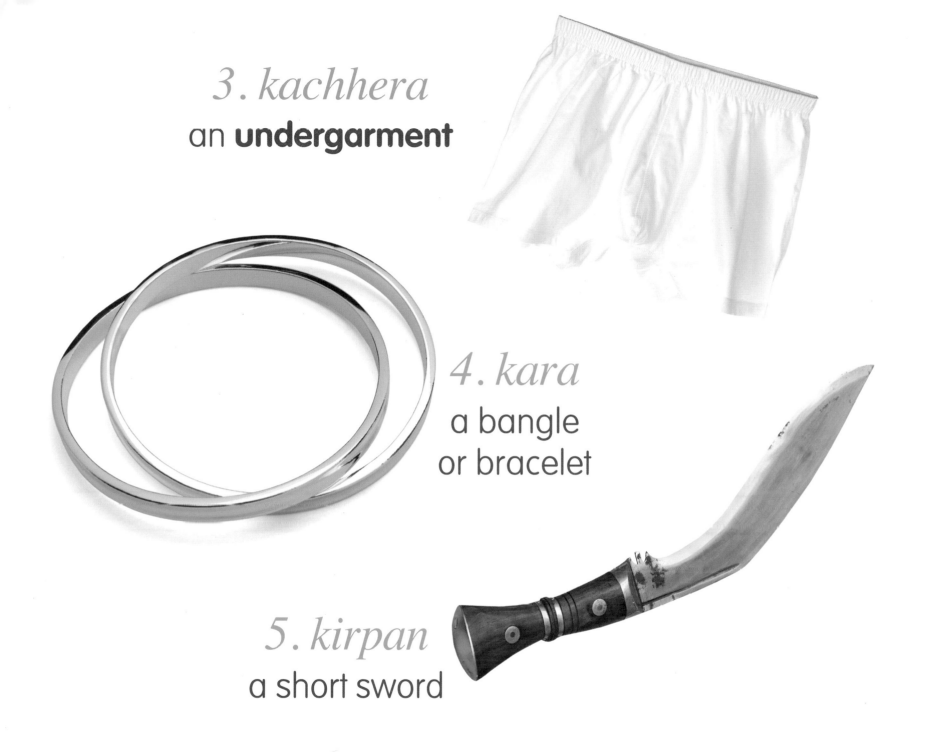

3. kachhera
an **undergarment**

4. kara
a bangle
or bracelet

5. kirpan
a short sword

When the Five K's are all worn together, it shows that
a Sikh person has made a commitment to the Sikh faith.

MARRIAGE

A Sikh wedding is called the Anand Karaj ceremony. The marriage can be held at any gurdwara.

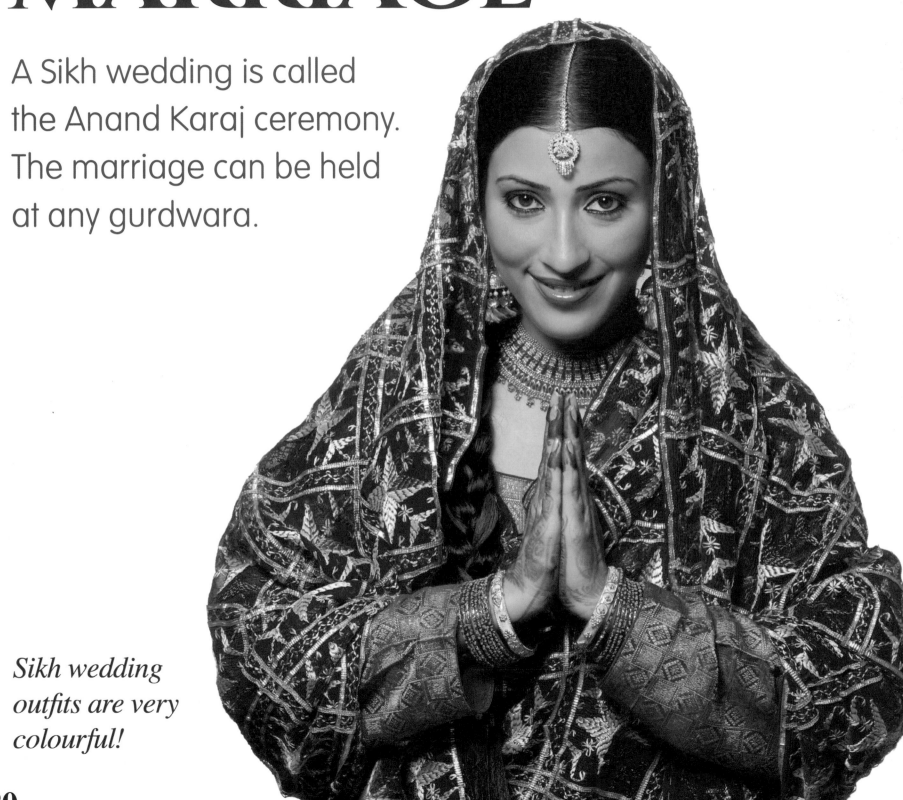

Sikh wedding outfits are very colourful!

Weddings usually take place in the morning and after the ceremony everybody eats together.

The wedding celebrations can last for two or three days!

Facts about SIKHISM

1 Sikh people do not drink alcohol.

2 Sikh people never cut any of their hair.

3 All Sikh men wear a turban, which is a long piece of material tied around their head. This shows commitment to their religion and also helps to keep long hair tidy.

4 The Guru Granth Sahib has its own bedroom and at night time it is wrapped up in blankets.

The top part of the Golden Temple is made from pure gold!

GLOSSARY

Ceremony acts that are performed on religious or social occasions

Festivals when people come together to celebrate special events or times of the year

Hymns religious songs that are sung to God

Undergarment something worn under clothes

Worship to show a feeling of respect